W9-CYH-128

DATE DUE

DEMCO

The Clover & the Bee

A BOOK OF POLLINATION

To make a prairie it takes a clover and one bee, —
One clover, and a bee . . .

Emily Dickinson

The Clover & the Bee

A BOOK OF POLLINATION

Anne Ophelia Dowden

Illustrated by the Author

HarperCollins*Publishers*

To Mildred and Albert Van Vlack,
dear friends who share with me
their plants, their knowledge,
and their enthusiasm

Some of the material in this book first appeared in THE SECRET LIFE OF THE FLOWERS, published in 1964 by Western Publishing. Those illustrations are now in the collection of the Hunt Institute of Botanical Documentation, Pittsburgh, Pa., which has kindly allowed me to use several of them again. Some of the orchid material appeared in *AUDUBON* magazine.

The hundreds of specimens on which these drawings are based were collected over many years, in many parts of the United States. I want to thank all the people who helped me to find them, especially Mr. and Mrs. Albert Van Vlack, Canaan, Conn., Mr. and Mrs. Frederick McGourty, Norfolk, Conn., and Mrs. Gertrude Foster, Falls Village, Conn. At the Brooklyn Botanic Garden, I received specimens, information, and generous aid from Dr. Stephen K-M Tim, Miss Marie Giasi, and Mr. Edmond Moulin; and at the American Museum of Natural History, Dr. Louis Sorkin kindly identified many of my insects. Most of all, I am indebted to Dr. Peter K. Nelson, Professor of Botany Emeritus, Brooklyn College, who provided answers for intricate botanical questions, read my manuscript, and gave discerning and invaluable advice.

Library of Congress Cataloging-in-Publication Data
Dowden, Anne Ophelia Todd, 1907–
    The clover and the bee : a book of pollination / Anne Ophelia Dowden ; illustrated by the author. — 1st ed.
        p.   cm.
    Includes indexes.
    Summary: Explains the process of pollination, describing the reproductive parts of a flower and the role that insects, birds, mammals, wind, and water play in the process.
    ISBN 0-690-04677-4. — ISBN 0-690-04679-0 (lib. bdg.)
    1. Pollination—Juvenile literature. [1. Pollination. 2. Flowers.] I. Title.
QK926.D68 1989   87-30116
582'.01662—dc19   CIP
                                                                      AC

Contents

GOLDENROD

LET US HAVE EYES TO SEE

"Let us have eyes to see
The new-old miracle . . ."

Pollination is one of nature's miracles. It is the beginning of all seed-making, the first step in the reproduction of all flowering plants.

For human observers, pollination is a matter of wonder and delight. No subject in the realm of nature is closer to the heart of life. None has more majestic implications—and none is more simply entertaining and downright amusing. All around us, wherever there are flowers, they are being pollinated, and in all our garden borders, along every country road, small dramas are constantly being acted out. To be an audience, we need only to stand and look. The players are appealing—flowers modest or spectacular but always beautiful, insects and other animals always interesting and often beautiful too.

I

It is very easy to join the audience. Insects work busily and seldom pay any attention to an onlooker, so we can get very close—even stroke a furry bumblebee. Watching the insects, we can see also the flowers' part in the action, and can spy on them as they open or close or move in response to their visitors. We can activate many floral mechanisms ourselves, with a pin. All this observing can be done with the naked eye, but a small hand lens will make some things clearer.

As we stand and watch, we get acquainted with both flowers and animals. We come to know the various insects—their "personalities" and their ways of going about their business. We learn the inner forms of flowers, recognize their family relationships, and identify the meaning of their shapes and colors and structures. All this is pure fun. And our pleasure increases as we gain knowledge of the whys and wherefores— the problems involved in the processes and the amazing devices nature has evolved for solving them. We begin to see great meanings behind the surface patterns, and realize that we are catching glimpses of nature's wonderful basic plans and biological rhythms.

This drama began when flowers first appeared on earth, and it has become steadily more complex as the world has evolved. Plants today sustain the living world, but they could not do this without the help of animals, and the fates of all living things are closely bound together. We live in this world as guests of green plants, so it is important that each of us knows that world and cares about it.

MUSK ROSE

THE FLOWERS

For the million years man has lived on earth, flowers have been the glory of the green world around him. Their blossoming delights us all, from the youngest child to the oldest philosopher. But they do not exist for our delight, and their great beauty, in spite of what poets say, is not "its own excuse for being." All flowers, large or small, dull or spectacular, exist for one purpose only—to make new plants.

Flowers are the reproductive organs of a plant. They bear the male and female cells, and they provide ways for those male cells to join those female cells in order to produce seeds. The shape and color of every flower, its scent, its texture, its opening and closing, all serve the precise and wonderful mechanisms by which plants reproduce themselves.

3

A TYPICAL FLOWER

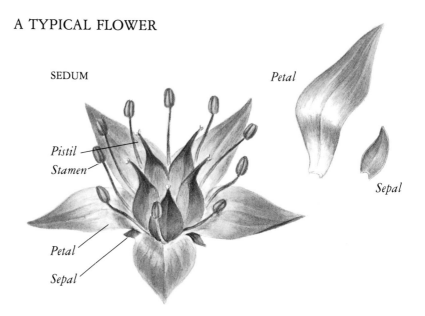

SEDUM

Petal

Pistil

Stamen

Sepal

Petal

Sepal

The basic plan of a flower is not hard to understand, and it is clearly visible in a simple blossom like that of the sedum. Any typical flower has four sets of parts gathered together on a *receptacle*, which is merely the enlarged top of a stem. In the center of the flower are one or more *pistils* surrounded by a ring of *stamens*, then a ring of *petals*, and on the outside, a ring of *sepals*. The petals as a group are called the *corolla*; the sepals form the *calyx*.

The calyx is commonly green, with leaflike sepals. Its chief purpose is to enclose and protect the unopened bud.

The corolla also shields the inner flower parts, but its most dramatic duty is to attract various agents of pollination, provide them with landing platforms, and guide them to pollen and nectar.

4

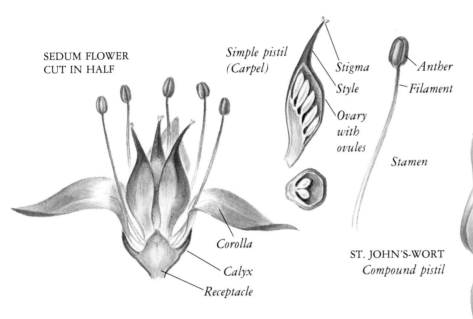

SEDUM FLOWER
CUT IN HALF

Simple pistil
(Carpel)

Stigma

Style

Ovary
with
ovules

Anther

Filament

Stamen

Corolla

Calyx

Receptacle

ST. JOHN'S-WORT
Compound pistil

Stamens are the male parts of the flower. Their little sacs, or *anthers*, hold, and finally release, *pollen* grains that produce the male sperm cells. These anthers usually grow at the ends of thin stalks or *filaments*.

The pistils in the center are the female parts. Each pistil usually has three clearly visible sections: At its base is the *ovary*, a pouch containing *ovules*; above this rises a stalk or *style*; and at the top of the style is the *stigma*, a sticky or furry knob that can catch and hold pollen. A basic simple pistil is called a *carpel*. In the sedum shown here, and in many other flowers, the carpels are all separate units. But very commonly carpels are joined together; several of them are fused into a single body, a *compound pistil*. The ovary is the part of a flower that becomes a fruit; the ovules become seeds.

5

All flowers have the same basic parts as the sedum, but in the vast world of plants, the variations on that pattern are infinite. Pistils are not only simple or compound; they also may be large or small, fat or thin, with stigmas tiny and knoblike or elaborately branched or feathered. Their styles may be long or short or even missing. Their ovaries may be plain round balls or complicated pouches, which may contain one ovule or thousands.

Flowers may have dozens of stamens or very few, often three or four or five. Their anthers are most often simple yellow sacs that shed pollen by splitting down the side, but they can be almost any shape and any color. The powdery

FIREWEED

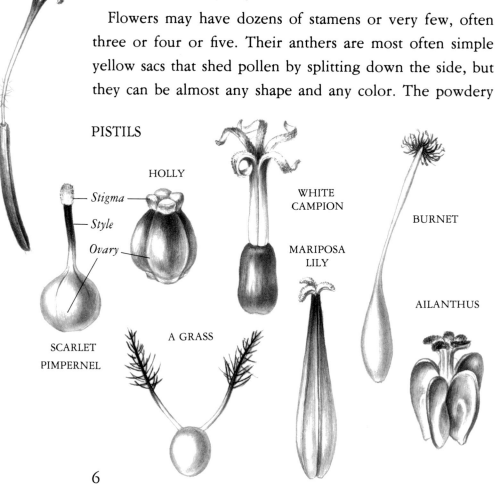

PISTILS

HOLLY

Stigma

Style

Ovary

WHITE
CAMPION

BURNET

MARIPOSA
LILY

A GRASS

AILANTHUS

SCARLET
PIMPERNEL

6

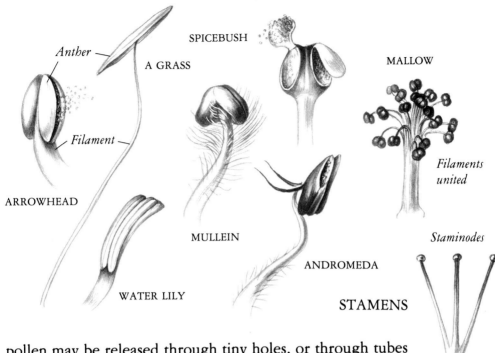

Anther

SPICEBUSH

A GRASS

MALLOW

Filament

Filaments
united

ARROWHEAD

Staminodes

MULLEIN

WATER LILY

ANDROMEDA

STAMENS

PARNASSIA

pollen may be released through tiny holes, or through tubes or "trap-door" windows. Filaments, like styles, are sometimes missing, or they may be joined together in various ways.

In some flowers, along with the stamens, we find *staminodes*. They may be merely sterile stamens that produce no pollen, but often they have peculiar shapes and a variety of uses, such as storing nectar or attracting insects.

Petals clearly are advertising banners, but they are much more than that. They shield pistils and stamens from cold and rain, and protect nectar. After attracting a visitor, petals give him a place to land and then influence his movements inside the flower. All the infinite variety of their colors and shapes and positions is due to the part they play in pollination.

CHRISTMAS
ROSE

7

PETALS AND SEPALS

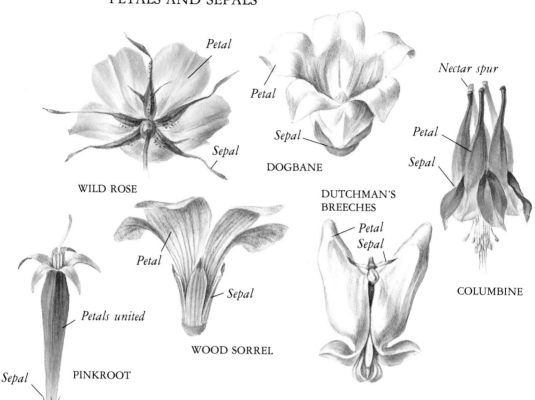

Petal

Petal

Sepal

DOGBANE

Sepal

WILD ROSE

Nectar spur

Petal

Sepal

DUTCHMAN'S
BREECHES

Petal
Sepal

COLUMBINE

Petal

Sepal

Petals united

WOOD SORREL

Sepal   PINKROOT

Petals, like stamens, can be many or few, as simple as those of a wild rose or as intricate as a columbine's. One or more petals may be joined together. They are often united into cups that may be bell-shaped, as in dogbane, or tubular, as in pinkroot; and they may have spurs that hold nectar. Often they are irregular in shape, with the ruffles and bright color patterns that attract pollinators. Or, in wind-pollinated blossoms, where such attractions are not needed, petals may be entirely lacking.

Sepals commonly match the petals in number. They usually

8

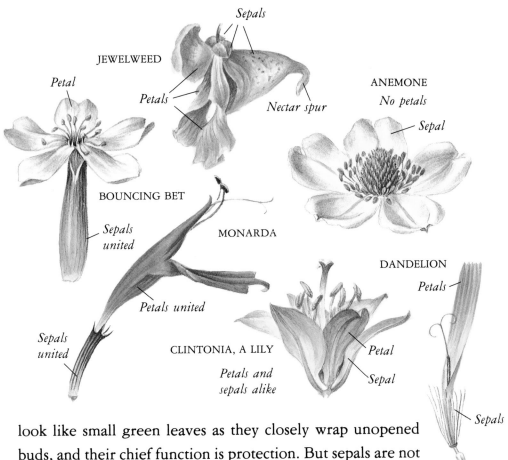

JEWELWEED

Sepals

Petals

Nectar spur

Petal

BOUNCING BET

Sepals
united

ANEMONE
No petals

Sepal

MONARDA

Petals united

Sepals
united

CLINTONIA, A LILY

Petals and
sepals alike

DANDELION

Petals

Petal

Sepal

Sepals

look like small green leaves as they closely wrap unopened
buds, and their chief function is protection. But sepals are not
always green, and they can vary widely in both shape and
color. They too may be united into bells and tubes, and sometimes they carry nectar spurs. In most of the lily family, they
look exactly like the petals. In the florets of the daisy family,
sepals have shrunk to a fringe of tiny scales or hairs, like those
of the dandelion. In the anemone and other members of its
family, petals are lacking and sepals replace them, with the
same look and the same duties.

9

POLLEN

Petals and sepals are so attractive that they often seem to be the essence of a flower. But they are, in fact, merely accessories, and the only absolutely essential parts are the stamens and pistils. It is their pollen and ovules that carry the beginnings of new plants.

Each tiny pollen grain has one purpose only—to find an ovule and deliver its male sperm nuclei to the female egg cells in that ovule. When pollen grains reach the stigma of a compatible pistil, they are caught in a sticky liquid and held there until they *germinate*. A tube breaks through the wall of each grain and grows down into the ovary. There it enters an ovule and releases two nuclei. One of these fuses with the egg cell of the ovule, which develops into a baby plant, or *embryo*. The other pollen nucleus unites with two more nuclei in the ovule, to develop into nutrient tissue. The ovule is now *fertilized*.

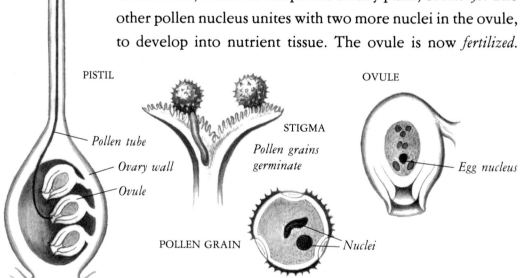

PISTIL

Pollen tube

Ovary wall

Ovule

STIGMA

Pollen grains
germinate

POLLEN GRAIN

Nuclei

OVULE

Egg nucleus

FERTILIZATION OF THE OVULE

Holding embryo and food tissue, it will become a seed, and the stamens and petals and sepals, their mission accomplished, can wither and drop.

Since, in most flowers, pollen-producing stamens grow close to ovule-bearing pistils, it would seem to be very simple for that pollen to fertilize those ovules. This *self-fertilization* sometimes happens, but it has a serious disadvantage—the loss of a mixture of heredity.

The patterns of heredity are carried by genes in the nuclei of both the pollen and the ovule. A mixture comes only when pollen of one plant, bearing a certain set of genes, unites with the ovules of another plant, with a different set of genes. This is called *cross-fertilization*. Such a union is possible only in plants of the same or closely related species. The pollen of a lily will have no effect at all on a rose. This mix of heredity produces offspring that are different from either parent. It enables plant species to improve themselves, to become healthier and more productive; and over many generations, it produces new species.

The naturalist Charles Darwin once said, "Nature tells us in the most emphatic way that she abhors perpetual self-fertilization." She has certainly gone to great lengths to prevent it—to make sure that each flower receives its pollen from another plant. Accomplishing this requires the aid of a great variety of mobile helpers, mostly insects and wind. And an almost unbelievable number of devices have evolved that prevent, or at least hinder, self-pollination.

The problems begin with the release of pollen. It bursts from ripe anthers in enormous quantities. There is enough so that thousands of grains can be eaten by insects and thousands more can die without reaching receptive stigmas. The individual pollen grains are so small that they can be seen only with a microscope, and they have a great variety of shapes. Pollen to be carried by the wind is light and smooth *Insect pollen* and hard-coated. It blows away quickly as the anthers split. The pollen carried by insects is heavy and sticky, often with spines or ridges that catch on the bodies of its carriers. It clings in powdery masses to open anthers until it is picked up. Insect pollen never floats in the air, and therefore only wind pollen causes hay fever.

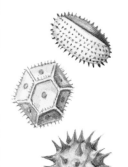

With so much pollen around, a plant has to have very efficient ways of avoiding its own pollen and making use of that from other plants. Usually a flower's anthers and stigmas grow in such a position that they can not touch each other. And in a great many plant species, the separation is even more decisive than that—stamens grow in one flower, pistils in another. Sometimes, as in castor beans and birch trees, these *staminate* and *pistillate* flowers are borne on the same stem. Sometimes, as in sassafras and white campion, they grow on entirely separate plants.

But the most common—and most effective—method of preventing self-pollination is a matter of timing: the anthers and stigmas of a flower do not ripen together. In some cases,

Wind pollen

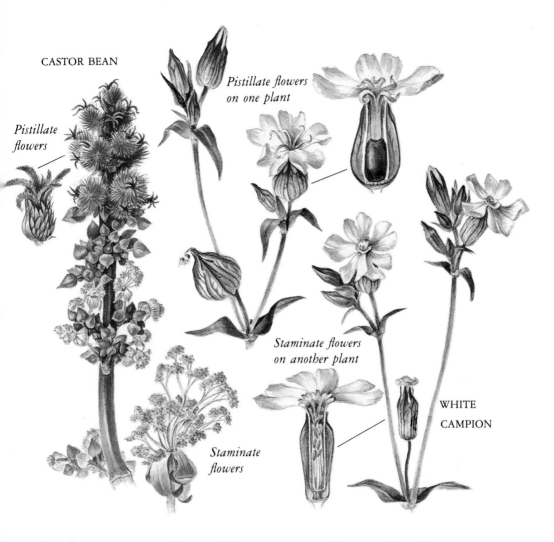

CASTOR BEAN

Pistillate
flowers

Pistillate flowers
on one plant

Staminate flowers
on another plant

Staminate
flowers

WHITE
CAMPION

the stigma matures first and becomes receptive to pollen before the nearby anthers have ripened. It can then be fertilized
only by pollen brought from an older flower, which has ripe
anthers. In other species, the opposite happens: the anthers
ripen and shed their pollen so that it is all carried off before
the stigma is ready to be fertilized. Thus each flower has a
female phase and a male phase.

1 Young flower

2 Anthers presenting pollen

3 Anthers empty, stigma ripe

PARNASSIA

Parnassia is a male-first flower. Its petals open to show five fat anthers pressed tightly around the small green knob of the undeveloped pistil, all surrounded by a fringe of staminodes. One by one, the filaments grow longer. Each in turn raises its anther above the center of the flower and holds it there to touch visiting insects. When its pollen has all been carried off, it moves downward and outward, to lie against the petals, while another anther takes its place above the pistil. Only after all the stamens have done this and the last pollen is shed does the stigma mature, spreading four fuzzy stigma-arms, ready to receive pollen.

Collinsonia is female-first. In a young flower, with the stamens still curled back in the flower throat, the long pistil holds out its ripe forked stigma even before the bud has fully opened. It catches any pollen brought by an insect and then it moves off to the side. After that, the stamens unroll and reach forward to dab pollen on later visitors.

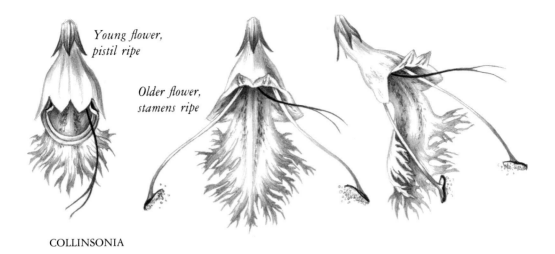

Young flower,
pistil ripe

Older flower,
stamens ripe

COLLINSONIA

Timing is a very good way of separating stigmas and pollen, but sometimes the methods are much more complicated. Some flowers have pistils and stamens of different lengths that must be matched to the pistils and stamens of another flower on another plant. In the Carolina jessamine, all the flowers on some plants have low pistils and high stamens. In other Carolina jessamine plants, the pistils are high and the stamens low. The insect that receives a dab of pollen high on his tongue will carry that pollen to the high pistil of a flower on another plant, and pollen from low-stamen flowers will be left on low pistils.

CAROLINA JESSAMINE
Flower cut open

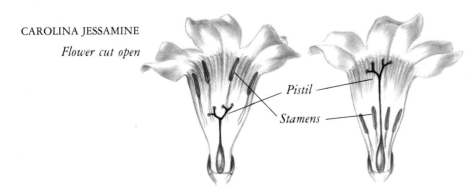

Pistil

Stamens

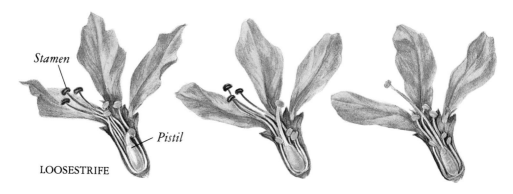

Stamen

Pistil

LOOSESTRIFE

Purple loosestrife has pistil-stamen sets of three different lengths. In these flowers, pollen from the longest stamens fertilizes the longest pistils. Pollen from medium-length stamens fertilizes medium-length pistils, and that from the shortest stamens fertilizes the shortest pistils.

We can easily see all these mechanisms, but there are invisible methods for preventing self-fertilization that are known only by laboratory testing. "Foreign" pollen usually takes precedence over a flower's own pollen. Thus, if a flower's pollen should fall on its own stigma at the same time that pollen also comes from another flower, the pollen from the other flower will be the one that germinates. And many flowers are self-sterile—their inner chemistry prevents their own pollen from germinating on their own stigmas. Some species reject their own pollen at first, but accept it at the end of their bloom, as a last-minute measure.

By all these ways and means, a pollen grain makes its way to join an ovule and start the life of a new plant, and all the intricate floral machinery exists for this purpose only. That is the whole meaning of flowers.

CLEARWING MOTH

DAME'S ROCKET

THE ANIMALS

When the first animals climbed out of the seas to live on land, they found the first plants already there. And so, during all their time on earth, animals have received food and shelter from plants. In the beginning, plants received nothing in return, but the coming of flowers changed that, and animals, especially insects, began at last to pay for food with service.

Of course, neither plants nor animals did this consciously. They both evolved by tiny steps over millions of years. Plant shapes and structures developed to fit the animals. The sizes and shapes and habits of animals changed, as well as the hairs on their bodies and the parts of their mouths. All this was directed by the balances of nature, by the laws of trial-and-error, of survival-and-extinction. And now, in our beautiful interlocking world, animals that carry pollen enable plants to produce seed, and many other animals help to distribute that seed. Thus they unknowingly propagate the plants they need for food and shelter.

Animal visitors usually come to flowers because they eat pollen or nectar or both. They collect and use this floral bounty in various ways according to their varied habits, but all animals, including insects, need protein for growth, and carbohydrates (sugar and starch) for energy. Pollen provides rich protein; nectar is almost pure sugar.

A great many animals live among flowers. Some are gathering food, some are hunters preying on other animals, some are seeking shelter. Any of them may carry some pollen from flower to flower, but they are not true pollinators unless they have certain characteristics. They must visit flowers constantly, making many trips and distributing pollen rapidly, so the visits must be a regular and necessary part of their daily lives. And they must have shapes and habits that cause them to pick up pollen and carry it on their bodies.

A wide range of animals does this, from insects to birds and bats and even mice, but the insects are by far the most important. All the insects we will consider here have three life phases: a *larva*, or childhood stage, when the baby insect is wormlike; a *pupa* stage, spent dormant in a cocoon or shell; and an active adult stage, when growth has ceased and mating and egg laying take place. Larvae, with their developing organs, must eat a lot of protein; adults need the energy from carbohydrates to keep their activity going. Most of the flying ones need a great deal. But a few kinds, with short adult lives, arrive at maturity equipped with stored reserves of food so great that they do not eat at all.

Nearly all flowers have acquired at least a few of these pollinating allies, as, over the ages, groups of plants and groups of animals have formed special partnerships. Serving

18

the animals, the plants are served as well; and the process has, quite incidentally, produced all the infinite richness and beauty of today's floral world.

HONEYBEES

Honeybees are far and away the most important pollinators. Their relationships with flowers are nearly perfect, and by studying them in detail we can learn about the ways and means, the problems and solutions, of all such partnerships.

Honeybees are *social insects*: They live in large colonies, and all the complicated work of a colony is organized in a most precise and intricate way. Originally, honeybees lived in hollow logs or caves, but now they are nearly all domesticated in boxes, or hives, set out by man. The colony in a hive includes thousands of bees, all children of one mother, the queen. A queen bee sees the outside world only briefly, when—newly hatched—she leaves the hive, flies about until she meets a male bee, or drone, and mates with him. Then she returns to the hive and spends the rest of her life inside laying eggs, as many as a million in her lifetime. She is constantly attended and fed by her daughters, the working bees. They also feed the drones, who do nothing at all except fertilize young queens.

Honeybees are highly intelligent. They recognize and remember flower patterns and blooming schedules, they are able to operate elaborate mechanisms, and they can communicate with each other. The workers in a colony are incessantly

HONEYBEES

FLOWERING QUINCE

active, performing the multitude of tasks in the hive. This means that they need immense amounts of nectar and pollen, as well as water, so food must be gathered constantly. The gatherers, or foraging workers, are the only honeybees most of us see, and they are the ones that are most important to flowers. They appear each year along with the earliest spring blossoms, after spending a quiet winter in the hive, nourished by stored honey. And they are still hard at work when the season ends in November. In all the months between, workers are flying ceaselessly and—quite literally—working themselves to death, often in a few weeks.

Honeybees live entirely on pollen and nectar, and a worker bee's body has evolved into a wonderful little machine for gathering this food. Her head, thorax, and abdomen have a thick coat of feathery hairs to which pollen clings easily. Attached to the thorax are four wings and six legs. Each of the two hind legs has, below the knees, a section that is broad and hollowed out and edged with a fringe of spiky hairs. These sections serve as baskets for carrying pollen. With combs on her other four legs, the bee brushes pollen from her body, moistens it, and packs it into the pollen baskets. She usually does this as she flies, but occasionally she perches on a leaf to clean herself, and one can clearly see her combing her long fur. Back in the hive, she uses the sharp little spurs on her middle pair of legs to pry loose the pollen masses in her baskets.

A worker bee collects the syrupy nectar with her mouth. She has strong jaws, which can bite and grind, but they are used for such jobs as shaping wax cells or preparing food for larvae. She drinks nectar with her *proboscis*, or beak. It is a long

HONEYBEE'S BODY

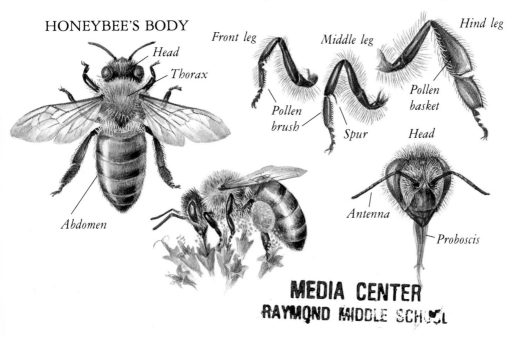

tube with a long tongue inside, kept folded under her chin when not in use. The bee can lap up small bits of liquid with her tongue, but if she needs to drink a lot, she sucks it through the tube like soda through a straw. The length of a bee's beak—about a quarter of an inch—is very important, because it determines how far she can reach into a flower for nectar. She drinks until the honey sac in her abdomen is full and swollen; then she returns to the hive and spits the nectar into a wax storage cell.

A bee's feelers, or antennae, carry her organs of touch and smell and, possibly, hearing. She uses them when she feels her way around inside blossoms or performs her many duties in the hive. And, as she flies, they bring her the scents of the flowers she wants to visit.

But, in general, sight tells her much more than smell does. A bee's keen eyes can detect moving objects, can tell light from dark, can distinguish shapes and patterns, and can recognize the difference in colors. Experiments have shown that bees see color much as we do, plus ultraviolet, which we cannot see. They are blind to red, but they respond to all the other hues and are especially attracted to blues and purples. They even like white flowers, which often reflect ultraviolet and, to the bees, appear to be colored.

When foraging for food, a honeybee moves rapidly and methodically, visiting every small floret on a stalk of thyme, for instance, until her abdomen is full of nectar and her legs are loaded with pollen. Then she flies home, deposits her

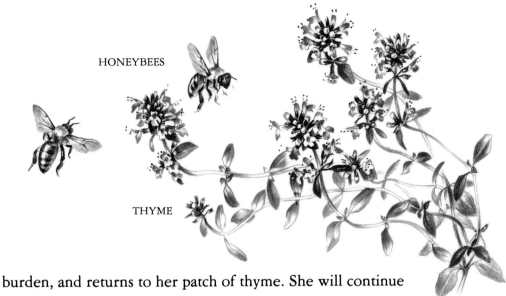

HONEYBEES

THYME

burden, and returns to her patch of thyme. She will continue to work on one kind of flower as long as it is available—often for many days.

If a foraging bee discovers a very rich food source, she will, on her return to the hive, tell her sisters what it is and where it can be found. She gives each one a taste of the nectar. Then with a little dance of turns and wiggles, she shows them whether the food is near or far, and what direction they must take to find it.

Honeybees are especially fond of the many flowers that have evolved to fit them. But they also gather both pollen and nectar from any blossom that is not too deep for their tongues' reach or too tightly closed for their strength. So these energetic workers are almost universal pollinators. A botanist has said, "Without bees to pollinate their flowers, one hundred thousand species of plants or more would perish from the earth. It seems to me a heavy responsibility for one kind of insect to carry."

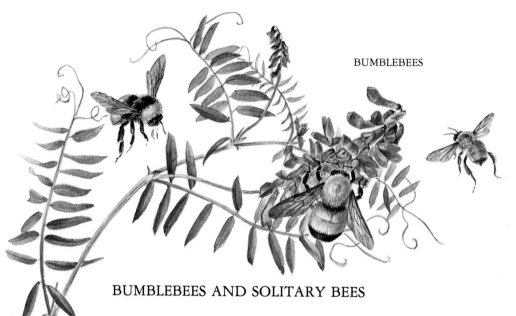

BUMBLEBEES

VETCH

BUMBLEBEES AND SOLITARY BEES

There are thousands of species of true bees in the United States, but as pollinators, honeybees outclass all the others. This is partly because none of those others have such a highly developed community life. Only a few of them live in communities at all, and their colonies are comparatively small. Most bee species are *solitary*, and their habits are very different from the habits of honeybees.

Of all the many kinds, the best known are certainly the bumblebees, which live in small colonies and are almost equal to honeybees in their usefulness to flowers. There are many species in the United States, of various sizes, but mostly much bigger and stronger than honeybees. Some have tongues three quarters of an inch long. They drink nectar and carry pollen on their legs as honeybees do, and they visit the same flowers, but they can also push their bodies into tightly closed blossoms and their tongues into deep floral throats.

24

A bumblebee's life is somewhat different from a honeybee's. Young queens appear in earliest spring, after hibernating during the winter in some snug hideaway, such as a hole in the ground or under a log. The colony where they were born has died out during the cold weather, but the queens were mated in the fall and are now ready to lay eggs. Each one finds a suitable nesting hole and starts constructing little cups or cells, laying eggs in them, and collecting pollen and nectar. In a month, she has a family of young workers to take over the labor of the group, and she settles down to a life of egg-laying. The colony grows, and in the late summer queens and drones are produced. They leave the nest and mate, the new queens dig in for the winter, and the rest of the colony dies. So bumblebees do not have to store winter food; but even so, they work almost as hard as honeybees.

No other bees are as familiar as honeybees and bumblebees, but we can easily meet many other kinds, of all sizes and all levels of intelligence. In the United States, most of them are solitary, and some are important pollinators.

Mining bees live in burrows in the ground, where each female, working alone, lays her eggs and stores pollen and

MINING
BEE

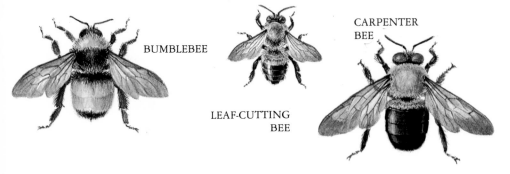

BUMBLEBEE

LEAF-CUTTING
BEE

CARPENTER
BEE

nectar. Her children remain sealed in their tunnels until their particular flowers bloom the following season. These bees have no pollen baskets and carry their loads on the long, branched hairs that cover their legs.

Leaf-cutting bees are common nearly everywhere, and they pollinate a great many flowers. They cut neat oval patches from leaves and paste them together into tubular cells, each of which holds an egg and a food supply. They also lack pollen baskets, but have instead a stiff brush of hairs on the undersides of their abdomens.

Carpenter bees are the most dramatic of our solitary bees. These giants—big as the biggest bumblebees—are mostly tropical, but a few species are found in the United States. They are vigorous performers and excellent pollinators.

WASPS

Wasps are close relatives of bees and in many ways closely resemble them. Some are solitary, living in tunnels in wood or earth, and others are social, building summer colonies that die in the fall, like those of bumblebees. But wasps differ from bees in a number of ways that make them far less effective as pollinators of flowers. Their bodies are generally smooth, and the hairs they have are simple and straight, not very good for carrying pollen. Much more important, wasps feed their young a diet of insects instead of pollen and nectar. The adults, with their great need for energy, live mostly on nectar, but they do not eat pollen at all, and much of their time goes

26

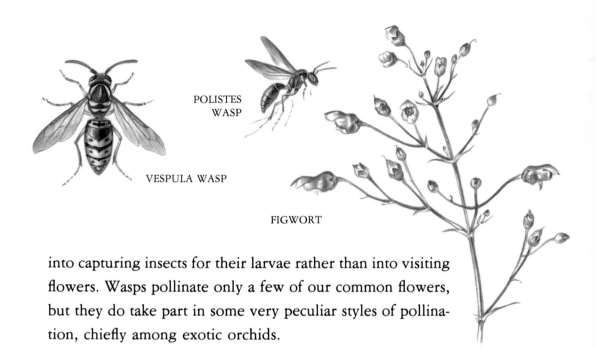

POLISTES
WASP

VESPULA WASP

FIGWORT

into capturing insects for their larvae rather than into visiting flowers. Wasps pollinate only a few of our common flowers, but they do take part in some very peculiar styles of pollination, chiefly among exotic orchids.

BUTTERFLIES AND MOTHS

Butterflies and moths are all good pollinators, even though they by no means rival bees. They live entirely on a floral diet, but they visit flowers only for the nectar they themselves eat, and they gather neither nectar nor pollen for their young. Their eggs are laid on plant stems and leaves, and the hatching larvae—the caterpillars—eat those leaves.

Butterflies and moths are closely related, and they differ more in habits than in body structure. They both lack biting jaws, but have very long tongues that are coiled like watch springs when not in use. Butterflies are active in the daytime, and—with very keen sight—they respond to flower shapes and colors rather than to scent. Unlike bees, they can see reds and seem especially fond of red flowers. When drinking, they

27

SWALLOWTAIL

ALFALFA
BUTTERFLY

SWEET WILLIAM

perch on the rims of flowers or on clusters of florets, and they drink most comfortably from tubes, long or short. Butterflies often visit tubular honeybee or bumblebee flowers, but their favorite blossoms have throats too deep for bees and other insects.

Most moths are night fliers, and the flowers they visit are night blooming, and light colored, with very strong fragrance. Moths do not perch on flowers while drinking nectar; they hover in front of blossoms, with wings beating rapidly, and thrust their tongues into the floral throats. Our largest and

28

HAWKMOTH

HONEYSUCKLE

most beautiful moths are rare, and some do not visit flowers at all, since they eat nothing during their adult lives. But we can often catch the medium-sized ones—the sphinx moths and hawk moths—at work in the twilight. And it is very easy to watch the few that fly by day, like the charming little clearwing. It visits butterfly flowers, but it moves like other moths, hovering to drink.

Both moths and butterflies are biggest and most glamorous in the tropics, where they occur in endless variety and pollinate some of the world's most exotic blossoms.

QUEEN ANNE'S
LACE

FLIES

Flies often look and behave so much like bees that it is hard to tell the two apart. But flies have only two wings, whereas bees always have four. There are thousands of species of flies, from mosquitoes and tiny gnats to big horseflies, but most of them live on animal material and only a few are connected with flowers. However, some of these few are excellent pollinators, mostly of simple blossoms, since complicated mechanisms are generally beyond their intelligence. They visit flowers only to feed themselves and do not, in fact, care for their young at all.

HOVER FLY

BEE FLY

HOVER FLY

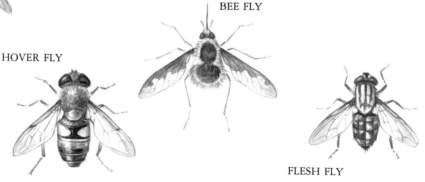

FLESH FLY

ROSE CHAFER

TUMBLING BEETLE

SOLDIER BEETLE

BEETLES

Beetles are very primitive insects, among the first to evolve and the first to pollinate plants. Today, most of them are scavengers or hunters, and the few that visit flowers eat the pollen of simple, shallow blossoms—and often eat the blossoms as well. These clumsy insects are not intelligent enough to find their way into deep or complicated flowers, they do not fly rapidly, and their bodies are too smooth to carry much pollen. So they pollinate only a few plants, many of which have trap flowers that take advantage of beetle stupidity.

LONG-HORNED BEETLE

ANTS

Ants are relatives of bees and wasps, but they are always considered the scoundrels of the floral drama. Though they love pollen and nectar, they are not good pollinators. Worker ants have no wings, and traveling on foot, they cannot move rapidly from flower to flower. Also, their shiny-smooth bodies do not pick up and carry much pollen. So they do not pay for what they eat, and plants have many protective devices, like closed throats or sticky hairs, that seem especially designed to shut these robbers out. Even so, there are two or three species of small plants, mostly in deserts, that are regularly pollinated by ants.

ANT

HONEYSUCKLE

RUBY-THROAT HUMMINGBIRD

BIRDS

In some parts of the world, birds do almost as much pollinating as insects do, and many plants are totally dependent on them. Birds' feathered bodies pick up pollen easily. They move around rapidly and constantly, and they have the intelligence for probing intricate flowers. They need great quantities of high-energy food, which they find in the easily digested sugar of nectar. However, they do not feed nectar to their chicks, and they almost never eat pollen. The protein needed by both babies and adults comes from insects, which the birds sometimes pick up in flowers, sometimes catch on the wing.

In the United States, hummingbirds are the only ones that

visit flowers. There are many species of these jewellike creatures, and they may be bumblebee-size or eight inches long. Their slender beaks are sometimes curved, sometimes quite straight, and may vary in length from a half inch to five inches. This beak does not touch the nectar: the very long tongue, thrust beyond the tip of the beak, sucks up the liquid. It is split for half its length into two forks, each one rolled lengthwise to form a tube like a drinking straw.

Hummingbirds are fantastic fliers, always on the wing, expending so much energy that they have to eat twice their weight of nectar every day. They drink from all tubular flowers, even small ones, but they can also reach into tubes too deep even for butterflies and moths. Hovering in midair like moths, they probe flower throats and receive big smudges of pollen on head or breast or back. Since hummingbirds have very sharp eyes and a poor sense of smell, their flowers usually lack fragrance and, instead, attract visitors with distinctive shapes and bright colors, especially red. A favorite hummingbird blossom is the odorless red honeysuckle, a relative of the fragrant white honeysuckle loved by night-flying moths.

HUMMINGBIRD TONGUE

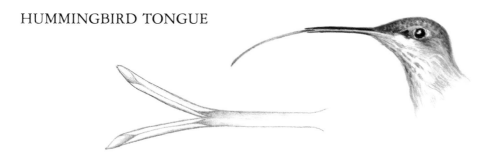

Europe has no bird pollinators, but elsewhere there are more than a thousand species, mostly in the belt of tropical forest that encircles the globe. In Africa and Asia, one finds sunbirds; in Hawaii, honeycreepers; in Australia, nectar eaters and brush-tongued parrots. Most of them are much bigger than hummingbirds, but they vary greatly in size and in the lengths and shapes of their beaks. And most of them perch to drink, on flower clusters or on nearby twigs.

BATS AND OTHER MAMMALS

As butterflies are replaced at night by moths, birds have their nighttime counterparts in bats. Most bats eat insects and a few eat fruit, but from both these groups a number of species have evolved into nectar eaters. They are mostly large, strong fliers, with long extendable tongues and very keen sight and smell, and their furry bodies easily pick up and carry pollen. Bats fly about at breakneck speed, stopping briefly to lap nectar. They can hover for only a few seconds, so they often cling to flowers with their claws, leaving them with tears and scratches. To withstand this rough treatment, bat flowers are usually large and tough.

Most bats in the United States are not flower visitors, but in our southwestern deserts, two kinds pollinate the giant saguaro and other cactus flowers. And in tropical areas, from South America to Australia, many plants depend entirely on bats. They include some of our valuable fruits like banana, avocado, mango, and guava.

Bats are the only mammals that do any important pollinating, chiefly because they are the only ones that can fly. However, in some parts of the world, many other small mammals roam through the trees and eat flowers. Most of them are merely destructive, but some do carry quite a lot of pollen on their fur and distribute it to the flowers they don't destroy. A rat in Hawaii does this, and so do some mice and monkeys in other regions. In Australia, a number of small marsupials live entirely on nectar and also distribute pollen. But neither these animals nor these plants have evolved any of the special adaptations that make a real pollination partnership.

SAGUARO CACTUS

LONG-NOSED BAT

THE PARTNERSHIP

The pollination partnership between plants and animals is a comparatively recent development in the life of our four-billion-year-old planet. The first plants that came out of the ocean 500 million years ago and gradually spread a mantle of green across the bare earth were like the algae and mosses of today. They reproduced themselves by means of microscopic sperms that wriggled their way through water to reach female egg cells. Variations on this method persisted through geologic ages, even after more complex plants developed.

Then conifers appeared—plants like pine and fir trees—with male sperm cells in pollen grains and female cells in small cones. The male cells were carried to the female cells by the wind. Finally, about 150 million years ago, flowering plants appeared, with their precise and efficient pollination and their protected seeds.

Insects too had been evolving. There were cockroaches about 200 million years ago and beetles a few million years after that. But the higher insects, like bees and butterflies,

36

appeared at about the same time as the flowering plants, and they all evolved together through the ages. So the pollination story is chiefly a history of insect-plant partnerships. In these partnerships, we find the most precise and marvelous adaptations in the living world. It seems miraculous that two lines of evolution—the plants and the animals—could mesh so perfectly, with such beautiful and practical resulting patterns.

All evolution proceeds by trial and error, as nature ceaselessly experiments. Some of her gene mixes and her accidental variations, or *mutations*, can make a plant stronger and more productive than its neighbors. Its offspring are likely to prosper. Thus, slowly, over many generations, new species are produced and existing species are changed to fit better into their surroundings. This is an age-old process, and it is still going on, although much too slowly for us to see it.

In all the long sequence of changes, no step was more important than the appearance of flowers. With their many advantages, flowering plants quickly dominated the vegetable world, and possibly nothing in the history of the earth so changed its face. No one knows for sure whether the very first flowers were pollinated by wind or by insects, or both. But the animal-plant partnership developed early, and it played a part in the floral takeover.

The beginnings were not, of course, conscious acts on the part of either the plants or the animals. It all started when a primitive insect, such as a beetle, blundered around in a blossom, eating petals and pollen. Then that insect unknowingly carried some pollen on its body as it visited another flower, to eat more pollen and pick up a new load. Gradually other insects evolved, with greater intelligence, greater skill, and new habits and needs. And flowers evolved at the same time, with devices that took advantage of insect skills. Some of the earliest and simplest flower types worked very well and have lasted to this day. But in general—with some exceptions and reversals—the trend of evolution has been from simple to complex.

All the complexities are the result of the flowers' need to attract pollinators and to use them when they arrive. Each species of plant does this in its own particular way. But all insect flowers have one or more of these characteristics: high visibility, scent, nectar, and abundant pollen.

A flower is highly visible when it contrasts with its surroundings. Bright-colored petals glow in the sunlight, and white ones stand out in moonlight. Large, elaborate petals attract attention, and small flowers can accomplish the same thing by joining with others in a cluster.

Scent is an important signal, especially useful for night-blooming flowers that are not easily seen. The sweet fragrances that we enjoy were created to please bees and moths and bats, but odors do not have to be sweet. Some flies and beetles visit flowers because a real stink—that of skunk cabbage, for instance—reminds them of the rotting flesh on which they lay their eggs.

In the beginning, pollen alone brought insects to flowers,

as it still does bring them. But then nectar appeared, and it became the most important of all attractants. Nectar is not, like pollen, a basic part of a plant's life process. It is of no use at all to a plant and is produced entirely for the animals. But possibly more than any other one thing, it has influenced floral evolution. Endless flower changes appeared in order to store nectar, protect it, advertise it, and ration it to visitors. And to drink it, insects developed sucking mouth parts instead of biting jaws.

In ancient flowers, nectar, like pollen, was openly displayed. It collected in drops on a pistil or in a little pool at the pistil's base. There are still flowers like this, but nectar is now more often produced and stored in *nectaries*. They grow on various parts of flowers and they can be almost any shape, from small shiny bumps at the base of the pistils to tubes

NECTARIES

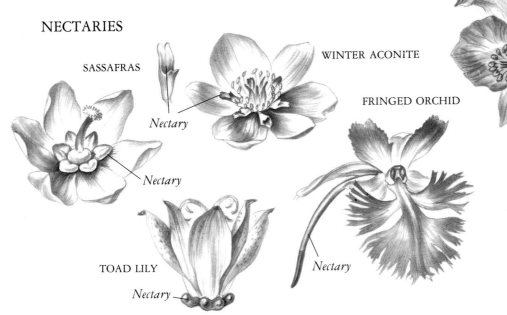

MONKSHOOD

Nectary,
a petal

SASSAFRAS

WINTER ACONITE

Nectary

Nectary

FRINGED ORCHID

TOAD LILY

Nectary

Nectary

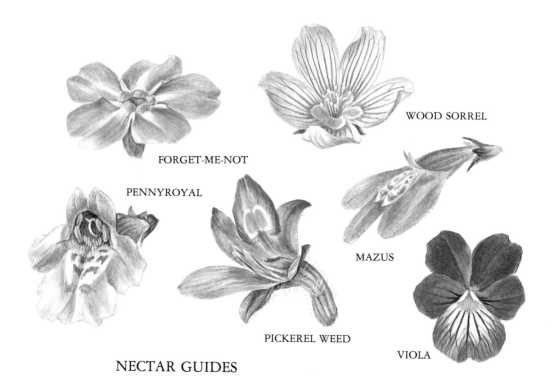

FORGET-ME-NOT

WOOD SORREL

PENNYROYAL

MAZUS

PICKEREL WEED

VIOLA

NECTAR GUIDES

several inches long. Access to them can be simple or extremely difficult, but usually it requires at least a little skill on the part of pollinators.

However, those pollinators are nearly always told where to find the nectar, if they have the wits to follow signposts. A bright circle may surround it, or a pattern of lines or of dots or even of odor may lead to it. These markings are called *nectar guides*, and they direct an insect quickly to its goal.

Hiding nectar has many advantages. When it is hard to reach, only good pollinators can get at it. And it is protected from loss or damage—from rain and wind, heat and cold, as well as from the nonpollinating animals that would like to eat

40

it. So there are many devices that shut out both weather and robbers. Narrow flower throats can do this, and so can throats filled with dense hairs or other obstructions, like those of partridgeberry and periwinkle, which permit the passage of a bee's tongue but not the body of an ant. And in some plants, robbers that come on foot are kept from reaching the flowers at all. They may be trapped on the plant stems by long woolly hairs or short sticky ones. Some plants sidetrack crawlers with drops of sweet liquid on their stems, in some cases producing this distracting syrup only while their flowers are in bloom.

One kind of theft is very common and very curious. Sometimes a lazy bumblebee goes to the outside of a tubular flower, bites a hole, and sucks the nectar through the hole. These bees steal not only from flowers with throats too long for their

DEVICES FOR PROTECTION

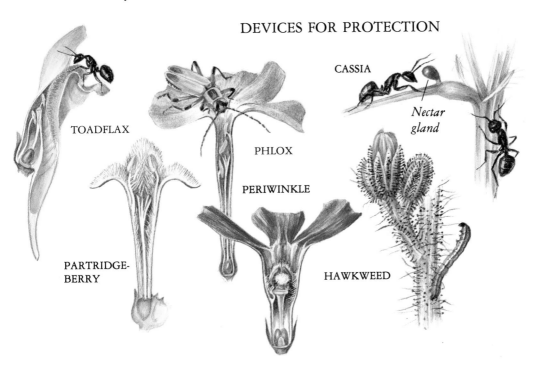

TOADFLAX

PHLOX

CASSIA

Nectar gland

PERIWINKLE

PARTRIDGE-
BERRY

HAWKWEED

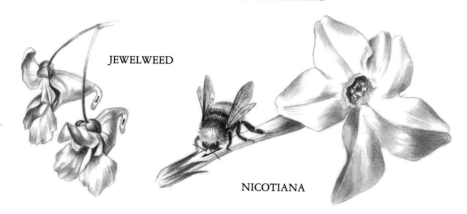

JEWELWEED

NICOTIANA

tongues, but also from flowers they could easily enter in the "correct" way. Thus they bypass all the machinery of pollination. And once such holes are cut, many other insects use them, even the most law-abiding honeybees.

All these devices for attraction, storage, and protection are part of the successful fertilization of flowers. They are therefore part of the pollination story. But the real drama in the story is the actual activity of animals and flowers—the way animals behave and the way flowers "take advantage" of them. The patterns begin with simple blossoms that welcome all comers equally and have no close partnerships with any. And they reach their peak of complexity in flowers so intricate that they can be pollinated only by a single species of animal. Between these two extremes are hundreds of fascinating variations. Those variations are all related to the ways pollen and nectar are stored and to the mechanisms that guide pollinators to them.

42

SAUCER FLOWERS

The earliest flowers were saucer-shaped or bowl-shaped, facing upward at the end of stems, like today's magnolia and water lily. In the beginning they had many parts—dozens of petals, stamens, and pistils—but gradually the numbers decreased, and now flower patterns are often sets of three or four or five. All the parts were at first simple in shape, simply arranged, with stamens and pistils in the center.

There are still many of these primitive circular flowers. All their petals are alike, and an insect can alight on any part, facing in any direction. Nectar and pollen are in easy reach, but finding them is accidental, since nothing tells the insect where to go. And picking up pollen for distribution is very haphazard. As an insect fumbles about, any part of his body can be smeared with it. Botanists call this the "mess and soil" method.

POPPY

WILD ROSE

MAGNOLIA

Some of these simple flowers, like their earliest ancestors, have no nectar. Wild rose and poppy, for instance, are pollen flowers only. But such blossoms have many visitors anyway, since pollen is a very popular food and they usually produce a lot of it.

Saucer flowers commonly are visited by beetles, the most inept of pollinating insects. But these flowers also attract all the less intelligent flies and wasps, and even some of the small solitary bees. Honeybees and bumblebees can drink from their shallow cups and often do, when there is no better choice available. But saucer flowers are quite useless to butterflies and moths and hummingbirds.

And they do not protect their nectar. After nectar appeared, flower shapes began to change. Petals gradually closed around pollen and nectar and acquired new forms and new functions that the old flat petals did not have. A great variety of new shapes evolved, many irregular and some very intricate. And often the whole flower grew differently on the stalk, tilting or drooping instead of facing upward.

All these floral characteristics influence the way an insect behaves when gathering food. He is invited to land in a certain place and then gently forced to follow a certain path, so that he accurately picks up a load of pollen on the way. In the next flower, following directions, he cannot avoid leaving that load exactly where it is needed. This pollinates the flower, but it also benefits the insect. He saves time in each flower and can make many more visits.

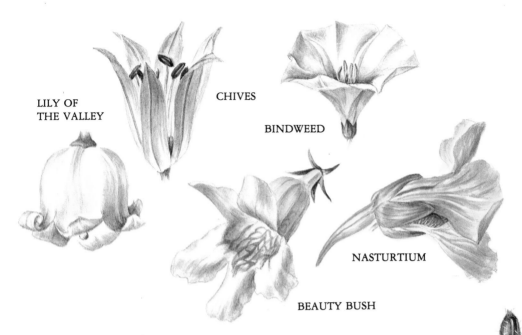

LILY OF
THE VALLEY

CHIVES

BINDWEED

NASTURTIUM

BEAUTY BUSH

COMFREY

BELL FLOWERS

Bell-shaped or funnel-shaped flowers are the first step in the trend. They may be shallow or deep, as simple as bindweed or as complex as beauty bush and nasturtium. Many bells are formed of petals joined together or, as in nasturtium, of joined sepals. Such flowers shield pollen and nectar much better than saucer flowers do. They do not shut out many visitors, but they make those visitors move in efficient ways. And they usually have special devices that deposit pollen in the right place.

The mechanism a bee finds in a campanula flower seems complicated. But it makes things easy for her, and in such a blossom her decisive action is very different from her aimless movements in a wild rose. When a campanula bud opens, the

45

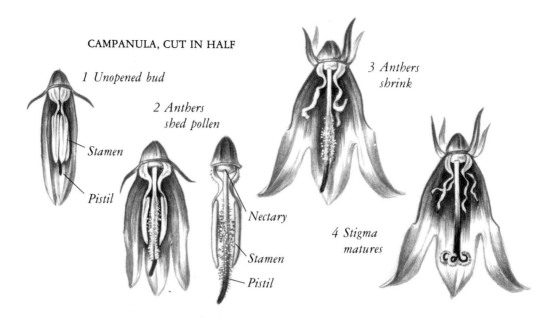

CAMPANULA, CUT IN HALF

1 Unopened bud

*2 Anthers
shed pollen*

*3 Anthers
shrink*

Stamen

Pistil

Nectary

Stamen

Pistil

*4 Stigma
matures*

pistil at its center is surrounded so completely by the five stamens that only its tip is visible. The swollen bases of their filaments enclose a ringlike nectary at the base of the pistil, and their anthers form a tube around the furry style. Soon these anthers split and shed pollen inside the tube, where it clings to the fur of the style but does not touch the tightly closed stigma. Then the stamens gradually shrink and finally curl back, leaving the pistil to stand alone, holding out its load of pollen. As the pistil grows longer, this pollen is in the path of all visitors. They always pick up some of it as they reach to the bottom of the cup and push their tongues between the stamen bases for nectar. Finally, the stamens are withered and the pollen on the pistil is all gone. Then at last, the stigma lobes open and stand ready to be fertilized by pollen brought from other, younger, flowers.

46

TUBE FLOWERS

It is only a step from the narrowest bell flowers to tube flowers, in which nectar is even more deeply hidden and access is more difficult. Such blossoms admit only a limited group of pollinators, but they have hundreds of devices that make the visits very profitable for the ones they do admit. Here we will find some of our most interesting flower-animal partnerships. In addition to deep, narrow throats, these flowers often have intricate shapes, with very definite landing places. And their machinery for picking up and depositing pollen can be very complicated. Those shapes and those mechanisms very neatly fit the bodies and motions of chosen groups of pollinators, as a mint blossom fits a bee.

With few exceptions, flowers of the big mint family are perfect honeybee flowers. Their nectar is stored in tubular throats that a bee can reach into or crawl into bodily. All of them tell her exactly where to go; most have honey-guides; and a great many are blue. A few mints, with bigger flowers and deeper throats, belong to bumblebees and butterflies; red monarda and scarlet sage are hummingbird flowers.

LAMIUM,
A MINT

HONEYBEE

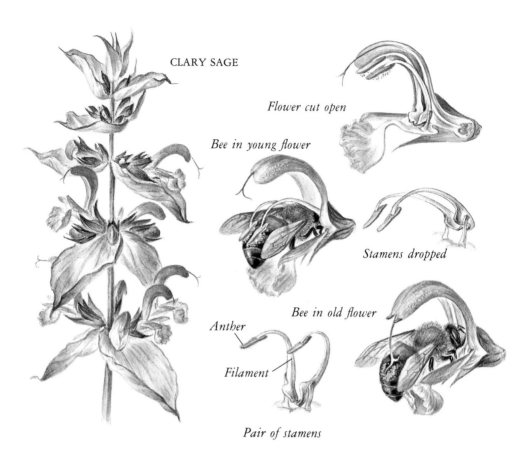

CLARY SAGE

Flower cut open

Bee in young flower

Stamens dropped

Bee in old flower

Anther

Filament

Pair of stamens

Clary sage is a common and interesting mint with a typical mechanism. Its large ruffled petal invites a bee to land, and she finds herself facing directly toward the nectar in the flower throat. As she moves forward, she inevitably touches the two curious stamens. Attached one on each side of the narrow throat, they are hinged in such a way that the filaments can swing up and down. As the bee's head pushes against their base, the upper ends drop, clamping their two anthers down onto her back and leaving a dab of pollen there. As long as

48

the flower has pollen to shed, the pistil remains out of the way, high against the upper petal. But when the pollen is gone, the pistil grows longer and hangs in the mouth of the flower in exactly the right place to pick up a bit of pollen from the back of a later visitor.

Flowers of the pea family also enclose their nectar tightly in narrow throats, although their petals are not joined to form a tube. All peas have a very distinctive shape, with five irregular petals. One petal rises above the others, large and showy, often with a bright nectar guide. The two lowest petals are always more or less united to form the *keel,* and inside the keel are the pistil and stamens. The filaments of the stamens, joined into a tube, enclose the pistil, and inside the tube, at the base of the pistil, is the nectar. To leave an entry for probing tongues, the topmost filament is separate from the others. But some peas have no nectar, an opening is not needed, and all their stamens are joined around the pistil.

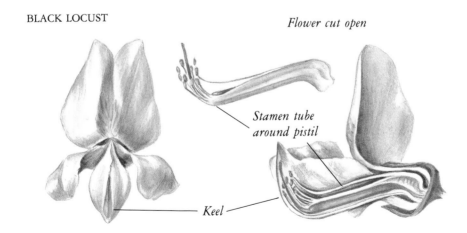

BLACK LOCUST

Flower cut open

Stamen tube around pistil

Keel

A bee alights on the keel of a pea flower and moves toward the nectar. As her weight pushes the keel down, the pistil and stamens are thrust up through the slit at its top, and they leave a dab of pollen on the underside of her abdomen. An insect that is not heavy enough or strong enough to depress the keel does not get any nectar or pollen.

Some peas, like Scotch broom, alfalfa, and tick trefoil, bombard the bee in a rather alarming way. They are trigger flowers, and their mechanisms go off with a small explosion. It is easy to see this happen in the common tick trefoil. If we gently thrust a pin where a bee would thrust her tongue, we may be startled as the flower seems suddenly to fly apart. The stamens and pistil have been held under tension inside the keel, and when they are touched, they snap out and up. They strike whatever is above them—usually a bee's stomach. The stigma, projecting a little ahead of the anthers, hits her first,

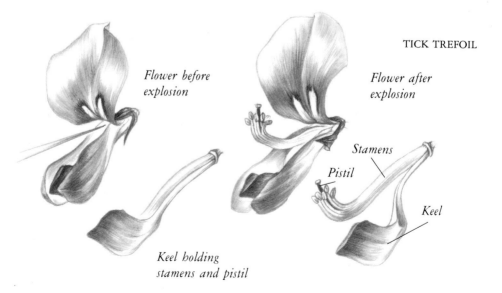

Flower before explosion

TICK TREFOIL

Flower after explosion

Stamens

Pistil

Keel

Keel holding stamens and pistil

WHITE CLOVER

Young flower

Old flower

so it catches any pollen she may be carrying when she arrives. Then the anthers hit her and leave a dab of pollen for her to carry to another flower. Once exploded, the trefoil does not close again.

These exploded flowers, of course, tell a bee which blossoms have spent their pollen and are no longer worth visiting—a great saving of her time. This is also done by other flowers in other ways. A great many pea flowers change color and position when pollen and nectar are gone. The depleted old florets in a head of white clover turn pink and droop. In a yellow currant, the center petals turn red after the flower is pollinated.

Flowers like mints and peas delight honeybees, but many of the larger tubular blossoms are quite out of bounds for bees and clearly belong to butterflies, moths, and hummingbirds. Cardinal flower, one of our most beautiful eastern wild plants, is a partner of the hummingbirds.

RUBY-THROAT
HUMMINGBIRD

CARDINAL FLOWER

In the cardinal flower—projecting forward from its center—there is a long beak with, at its tip, a knob and a little beard of stiff hairs. This beak holds stamens and pistil, but in a young flower we can see no signs of either until we cut it open. Then we find that the anthers are joined to form a tube, inside which they shed their pollen. Out through the center of the tube grows the pistil. Its tip is blunt because the two receptive surfaces of its forked stigma are pressed tightly together. And around its "neck" is a little ruff of stiff hairs.

As the style grows longer, the stigma is pushed slowly

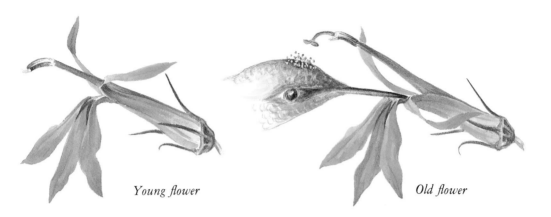

Young flower   *Old flower*

forward. Its collar of hairs fits the anther-tube perfectly, like a bottlebrush in the neck of a bottle. It shoves the mass of pollen ahead of it, out the end of the anther-tube, to rest on the shelf formed by the little beard. There the pile of pollen remains until it is brushed off by the head of a drinking hummingbird. Finally, when the pollen is gone, the pistil end itself emerges. Only then does the ripe stigma open its two lips and hold them in the path of another visitor, ready to receive any pollen the bird may be carrying.

STAMEN TUBE

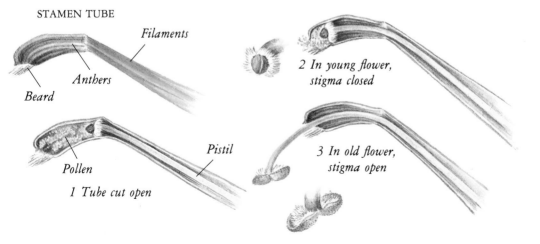

Filaments

Anthers

Beard

Pollen

Pistil

1 Tube cut open

2 In young flower,
stigma closed

3 In old flower,
stigma open

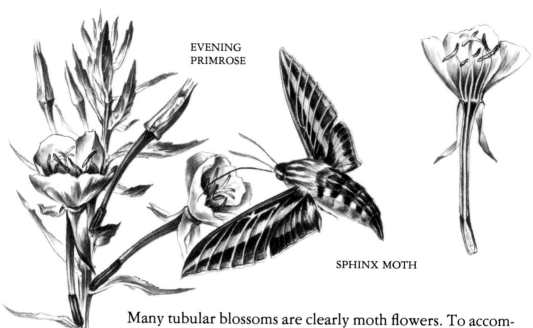

EVENING
PRIMROSE

SPHINX MOTH

Many tubular blossoms are clearly moth flowers. To accommodate the hovering moths, they stand out from their stems, as bird flowers do. But they are night blooming, and many—like evening primrose—open each evening and close in the morning. To be visible at night, they are light colored, often pure white, but mostly it is their strong fragrance that attracts their visitors.

Butterflies also prefer to drink from narrow tubes, and they pollinate most of the day-blooming flowers that store nectar in deep, thin throats. Phlox is a typical one, with its bright color, its long tube, and its ring of petals to serve as a perching place for the insect.

But butterflies also visit very small tubular flowers, and they are delighted by the ones in the heads of the Composite, or daisy, family. In this family, very tiny florets become highly visible because hundreds of them are grouped into dense

CABBAGE
BUTTERFLY

WILD PHLOX

clusters, or heads. Each head looks like a single flower and functions like one.

In the head of daisy or a sunflower, there is a central mass composed of tiny tubular *disk florets* tightly packed together. They hold a lot of pollen and nectar and can make a lot of seeds, but they might not attract insects if they were not surrounded by a bright ring of *ray florets.* These rays, tubular at their bases, spread out to look like petals.

OX-EYE DAISY

Disk floret

Ray floret

SILVERSPOT BUTTERFLY

Floret

SALSIFY

In some composites, like thistle, the disk florets are larger and brighter, and there are no ray florets. Other composites, like dandelion, have only ray florets. But all of them hold their nectar and pollen in narrow tubes. The smallest ones, like those of goldenrod, are so tiny that even very small insects can drink from them, and goldenrod sprays are nearly always covered with a variety, from little beetles to butterflies. The florets of large composites, however, have much deeper throats, and many are accessible only to bumblebees and butterflies. Butterflies can easily perch on the large heads, and they love nearly all composites.

All narrow throats are clearly good devices for controlling the movements of insects, but tubular passageways are not limited to flower throats. The iris shows us that other parts of a blossom can also form a tube. In irises, the three erect petals are often less showy than the three sepals. The bee is attracted by a large drooping sepal, with clear lines leading to its arched base—the path to the nectar. From the center of the flower, the large pistil spreads its three branches. Each branch, curving over a sepal arch, forms a tunnel, and has at its outer tip a double frill that conceals a stigma. Under each branch is hidden a stamen, pressed against the roof of the tunnel. As the bee follows the nectar guides through the tunnel toward the center of the flower, her back is smeared with pollen from the anther above her. Then when she visits another flower, the pollen is scraped off by the stigma at the entrance of the tube.

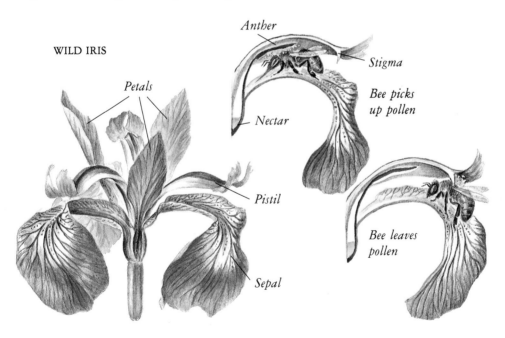

Anther

WILD IRIS

Petals

Stigma

Bee picks up pollen

Nectar

Pistil

Bee leaves pollen

Sepal

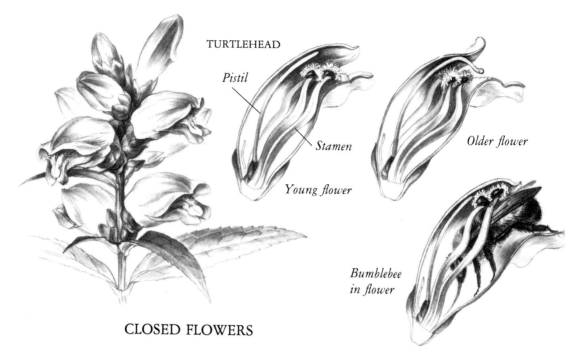

TURTLEHEAD

Pistil

Stamen

Young flower

Older flower

Bumblebee in flower

CLOSED FLOWERS

In all these narrow throats and complicated tubes, nectar and pollen are very well protected. But some floral types even go a step beyond that and close the mouth of the tube. Such flowers can be entered only by very strong and very intelligent insects. This usually means bumblebees, and most of the closed blossoms, like toadflax, bottle gentian, and turtlehead, are bumblebee flowers.

Of course, all these closed flowers finally welcome their visitors and are pollinated very precisely. Entering such a blossom and finding its nectar has to be done in a very definite way, which brings the body of the visitor exactly in the right place to pick up and distribute pollen.

On turtleheads, bumblebees work energetically. They push into flower after flower and depart from each blossom with a funny flip of their hind legs, as they comb pollen from their backs. To collect that pollen, the bee pries apart the flower's closed lips and crawls into a small chamber that fits her perfectly. This chamber, in a young flower, holds the pistil high against its roof. Below the pistil, two pairs of stamens clasp the bee like a little harness, their woolly anthers smearing pollen on her back. Although she combs herself as she leaves, she never removes all the pollen, so some of it still clings to her back as she enters an older flower. Here the pistil has grown downward and is in just the right position to touch the spot of pollen she carries. In a very old turtlehead, the pistil continues to grow until it curls back under the stamens. Then it can pollinate itself if no bee has done the job. These old flowers also turn pink at the tip, which of course tells approaching bees not to waste their strength on the spent blossom.

Blossoms like these very firmly shut out most visitors and can be considered exclusive bumblebee flowers. So too can red clover, a pea that is in effect a closed flower since it wraps its nectar and pollen so tightly that few insects can reach them.

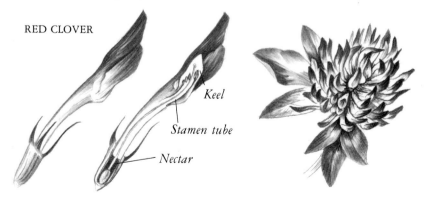

RED CLOVER

Keel

Stamen tube

Nectar

When European settlers first introduced this plant to New Zealand as a pasture crop, it failed to produce any seed because New Zealand had no native bumblebees. Farmers were able to grow their clover only after importing the bees from Europe and America.

TRAP FLOWERS

Closed flowers do not always gently guide visitors to nectar. Some of them are almost sinister, with traps that lure victims and then hold them captive until pollination is assured. Several members of the Dutchman's-pipe and arum families do this, preying chiefly on insects of low intelligence, especially carrion-eating flies and beetles. These trap flowers often send out an odor of decayed flesh, promising the insects—falsely —a good place to lay eggs.

One of these trap flowers is the spotted arum, or cuckoopint, an English cousin of our Jack-in-the-pulpit. Its large outer sheath, or *spathe*, encloses a vertical rod, the *spadix*. The spadix bears at its base a cluster of tiny pistillate flowers and, a little higher up, a cluster of staminate flowers. The tubular interior of the spathe is blocked in two places. In the narrow part above the stamens, the tube is filled by a fringe of hairs, which grow from the spadix with their points slanted downward. Then, between the stamens and the pistils, there is another, similar, ring of hairs.

The pistils mature first, and soon a flock of tiny flies, or midges, arrives, attracted by a foul odor. They can pass down

60

between the hairs to the base of the spathe, where they crawl about over the pistils and leave any pollen they may have brought from other plants. But when they are ready to leave, the path is blocked by those down-pointing hairs, and there they must stay until the stamens above have ripened. Then the lower ring of hairs withers and falls off, and a drop of nectar appears on each pistil as a reward for the impatient flies. But they cannot yet leave; the upper ring of hairs still holds them in the spathe. Buzzing around, they brush against the now open stamens, or crawl through pollen that has dropped to the floor of the chamber. So they are well dusted when the upper hairs finally shrivel and allow them to fly off to another flower and another captivity.

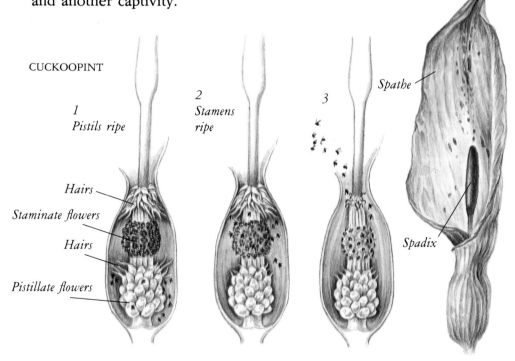

CUCKOOPINT

1
Pistils ripe

2
Stamens ripe

3

Spathe

Hairs

Staminate flowers

Hairs

Spadix

Pistillate flowers

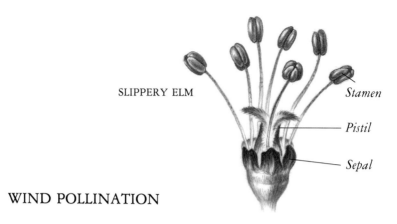

SLIPPERY ELM

Stamen

Pistil

Sepal

WIND POLLINATION

Exquisite partnerships with animals are responsible for so much of the beauty and drama of flowering plants that we are inclined to forget that there are also partnerships with the wind. Wind pollination existed before flowers did, and it is now considered primitive; but vast numbers of plants still use it—even some highly evolved flowering plants that may once have been insect pollinated. A few use both methods; willows and maples, for example, release their pollen to the wind, but their flowers also have nectar that attracts insects.

Wind flowers are quite different from insect flowers. They are nearly all very small, and their delicate beauty can often be seen only with the help of a lens. They have the familiar flower parts, but those parts have acquired special shapes in response to special needs, or—no longer needed at all—have vanished. Wind flowers lack all the devices that signal to insects: bright colors, scents, and tasty nectar. And of course they need no landing platforms or nectar guides. Thus petals serve little purpose, and they can even cut off air currents that carry pollen. So they are usually small and dull in color, very often green or greenish yellow. And very often they are missing entirely. Sepals are often small too, but they are sometimes thick and tough, since many of these flowers bloom in early spring and need to be protected from cold.

Stamens and pistils, on the other hand, must be large and prominent. Anthers dangle in the air on long filaments or else grow on long flexible catkins that move in the slightest breeze. Pistils spread feathered or ruffled stigmas to catch and hold passing pollen, and often they stand upright at the ends of twigs, waiting for pollen to fall on them.

Anthers open when the weather is warm and dry and breezy, and their pollen is quickly blown away. A gentle wind distributes it evenly, but rain washes it out of the air and also damages the tiny grains, so at the first raindrop, anthers quickly close. Their pollen grains are extremely smooth and light; some even have minute air sacs that help them float.

TIMOTHY,
A GRASS

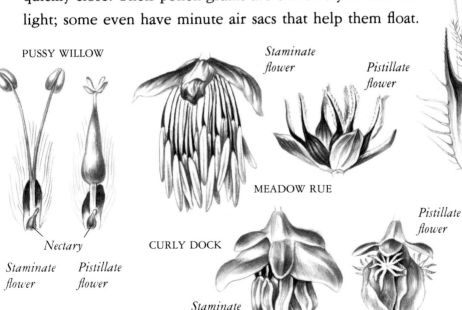

PUSSY WILLOW

Staminate flower

Pistillate flower

MEADOW RUE

Nectary

Staminate flower

Pistillate flower

CURLY DOCK

Staminate flower

Pistillate flower

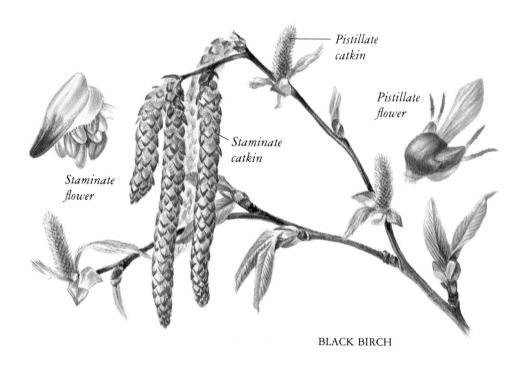

Pistillate catkin

Pistillate flower

Staminate catkin

Staminate flower

BLACK BIRCH

Wind flowers release amazing amounts of pollen. It spreads in yellow clouds from a jiggling catkin or a waving grass spray, or piles up on the ground beneath a blossoming tree. Cattail spikes shed pollen by the cupful. But although these amounts are enormous, the loss is great too, and the number of pollen grains that actually find their targets is small. The ones that reach stigmas would not be enough to fertilize many ovules, and wind flowers have very few—one ovule only in each flower of walnut, dock, and grasses; only two in birch and alder flowers. In contrast, insect-pollinated lilies have hundreds of ovules in each ovary, which means hundreds of seeds from each flower.

64

At first sight, wind pollination would seem to be extremely inefficient. Pollen released in vast amounts, then carried at random through the air until it reaches a receptive stigma of its own species—this is a truly hit-or-miss operation. But these drawbacks are overcome by the sheer quantities—the millions of tiny florets, the clouds of flying pollen. In the spring the air is filled with pollen of trees and grasses, and in the fall with that of plants like ragweed.

Wind plants grow in large colonies and bloom early or in open places, so that thick foliage does not hinder the movement of pollen through the air. In dense tropical jungles, where leaves never fall, there is no wind pollination. But it is very common in the springtime forests and the open prairies of the north. Nearly all our trees and grasses are wind pollinated, and grasses are probably the most important family in the vegetable kingdom—of all common plants, the most common. Wind pollination is certainly not outmoded.

WATER POLLINATION

Wind and animals pollinate nearly all the flowering plants in the world, but there is a tiny number served by a different agent—water. These flowers are truly strange, because water is usually the enemy of pollen. Most plants that grow in water are pollinated in the air; the flowers rise above the surface and are visited by insects or wind. But in a very few cases it is water that carries the pollen to the stigmas, and the familiar aquarium plant, vallisneria, or ribbonweed, is one of them.

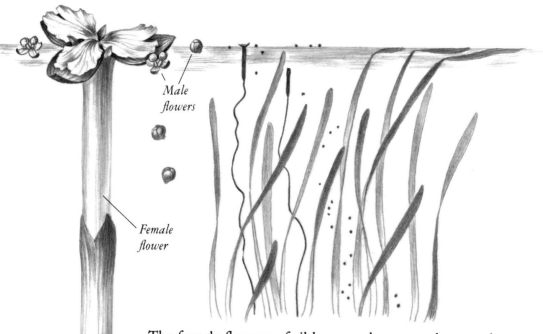

Male flowers

Female flower

The female flowers of ribbonweed grow on long corkscrew stems up to the surface of the water, where they open and spread their three-part stigmas. Male flowers, borne in clusters on short underwater stems, break off one at a time, float to the surface and open there. Their turned-back sepals serve as tiny rafts, holding up the stamens until they bump against a stigma and the jolt of the collision scatters their pollen on it. After pollination, the stem of each female flower coils up in a spiral, pulling the blossom down again under the water. There it forms its seeds close to the bottom of the pond.

RIBBONWEED

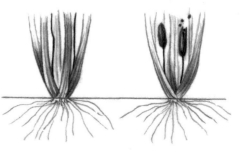

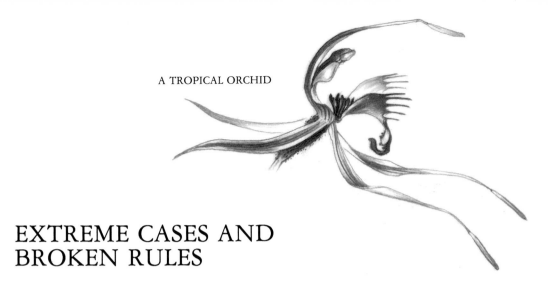

A TROPICAL ORCHID

EXTREME CASES AND
BROKEN RULES

All these intricate relationships between flowers and their pollinators are the result of ages of nature's trial and error. Floral patterns and insect skills have become steadily more precise, and now all flowers are pollinated by suitable agents. Most flowers have a variety of agents, and most animals gather food from a variety of blossoms, but in a few cases, one plant and one animal have become perfect and exclusive partners. This results in very efficient pollination, but it has its dangers: if some change in environment should destroy one partner, the other would perish too. Such disasters have caused the extinction of many plant and animal species. They have also led to regular self-pollination in some plant families. But in spite of their dangers, these exclusive partnerships are the peak of plant evolution, and most of them work beautifully. Other highly evolved and extreme pollination systems are interesting because they are unbelievably complex, with truly bewildering mechanisms.

One of the exclusive partnerships is that of the yucca, or

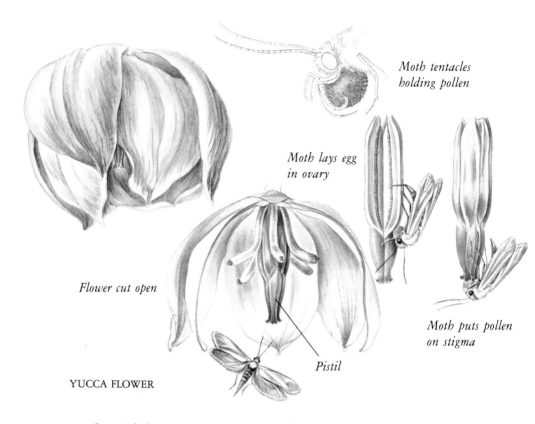

Moth tentacles
holding pollen

Moth lays egg
in ovary

Flower cut open

Moth puts pollen
on stigma

Pistil

YUCCA FLOWER

Spanish bayonet, and a small female moth. Yuccas grow wild in the southwestern United States and Mexico, and a few species are found in gardens elsewhere, all bearing tall handsome stalks of drooping white or pinkish flowers. The yucca's little white moth, less than an inch in wingspread, has two very unusual features: parts of her mouth have developed into a pair of spiny tentacles, and the egg-laying tube at the end of her tail—her *ovipositor*—is a horny spike.

The little moths emerge from their cocoons just as the yucca flowers begin to bloom. Soon each female has mated and is ready to lay her eggs, and in the twilight she flies among

68

the tall spires of opening yucca flowers. From each of them she collects pollen and carries it in her tentacles, rolled into a little ball under her chin. When the ball is several times as big as her head, she flies to still another flower and goes directly to the pistil at its center. Here she thrusts her sharp ovipositor through the wall of its ovary and deposits three or four eggs inside. This done, she climbs to the tip of the pistil and pushes her ball of pollen into the fork of its stigma, carefully rubbing it in.

This pollen is not food for her larvae nor for herself. (She does not eat at all during her short adult life.) It is purely for the benefit of the flower. Thus fertilized, the flower's ovary will grow into a large pod holding hundreds of seeds. When the moth larvae hatch inside it, they will feed on the seeds, but even when there are several larvae in a pod, the plant can easily afford the loss. Eventually each larva bores a hole through the wall of the pod, drops to the ground, and passes its pupa stage buried there for the winter. Next summer, it will emerge as an adult just when the yucca flowers start to bloom.

YUCCA SEED POD

Holes made by larvae

This little moth directly arranges the fertilization that is necessary to produce the seeds her offspring need to eat. In the whole field of pollination, it is the only case in which an insect "deliberately" fertilizes a flower for the good of the plant and the future benefit of babies she will never see, and not as an accidental part of her own food gathering. No one knows what started such a habit or how the moth's curious body developed. But the partnership must be very old, since many species of yucca have evolved and, with only one exception, each has a species of *Tegeticula* moth that has evolved with it. Yucca flowers still produce nectar—useless to the moth—and are visited by a number of other insects. But none of those insects play any part in its pollination, and the yucca depends entirely on its little moth.

Milkweeds, on the other hand, are not at all exclusive. They are visited by a surprising variety of insects. But the machinery that makes use of those visitors is one of the most intricate in the plant kingdom. Milkweeds are among the commonest

MILKWEED PODS

of North American wildflowers. Almost every section of the United States has some members of the group, handsome plants with wonderfully fragrant flowers. The biggest and commonest one has clusters of dull pinkish florets, and its big seedpods are more admired than its blossoms. Nearly everyone knows these beautiful pointed pods, with masses of dark seeds carried on silky white parachutes.

It is easy to find milkweeds, and easy to watch their pollinators at work on them. But it is not at all easy to understand how their various parts operate. A flower cluster of a common milkweed may have nearly a hundred florets. Insects, attracted by their fragrance and plentiful nectar, are met by a set of confusing mechanisms, a puzzle of interlocking structures. Each small floret holds up to the visitor, not petals and sepals (these are turned down, out of the way), but a little crown, or *corona*, of five nectar cups. If we remove the corona, we find a bumpy knob—the stigma closely clasped by five anthers.

MILKWEED
FLOWER

Corona

Petals

Nectar cup

Pistil

Stigma

Anther

Sepals

MILKWEED FLOWER

Bee picks up pollinia

Anthers clasping pistil

Inner side of anther with pollinia

An insect, coming to drink from a nectar cup, usually grasps the crown, and very often some of its feet slip into the tiny slits between the cups. When it flies away, it pulls its feet from the slits and carries on them one or more pairs of strange little yellow blobs.

We can duplicate this by pushing the point of a pin into one of the slits, just below the minute black dot at its top. When the pin is pulled gently upward, it will come out at the top of the slit like the leg of a departing insect. And it will carry a pair of *pollinia*—waxy masses of pollen connected by slender arms and a black shiny disk. They are so small that it is hard to see them without a hand lens. Then, if we continue as an insect would, we will push our pin into a similar slit on another flower and again pull it upward. The pollinia will be dragged after it and will be rubbed against the stigma hidden inside the slit.

This stigma is almost completely enclosed by the strange anthers that surround it. Each anther has on its inner face two pockets, which hold the two pollinia until they are pulled out by the leg or tongue of an insect.

Sometimes insects, especially the weak ones, are caught so tightly in the slits that they are trapped and held until they die. But most visitors have no trouble, and milkweed flowers are great favorites with all kinds of insects.

Milkweed pollination is certainly successful, since milkweeds often take over whole fields, spread by thousands of silk-borne seeds released from the big pods. Each sturdy plant bears only two or three of these pods. This is quite enough, but it is rather surprising in view of the hundreds of flowers that preceded them on those same stalks.

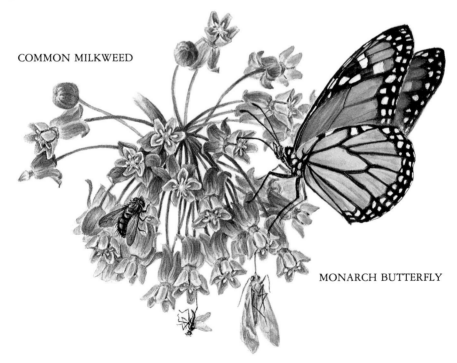

COMMON MILKWEED

MONARCH BUTTERFLY

Even milkweeds are no match for the orchid family in the complexity and strangeness of their pollination systems. Orchids, aristocrats of the vegetable kingdom, have reached the very peak of floral evolution. They seem to use every possible pollination device, and many have exclusive partnerships with single pollinators. This may have led to the extinction of some orchid species, but the family as a whole prospers—from the tropics to the arctic.

All this intricacy and variety of pollination has of course produced an equal variety of flower shapes. Although some orchids look like typical flowers, many have strangely elongated or twisted petals, beards and fringes, and peculiar color patterns. But their basic parts are the same as those of all flowers, not really hard to understand.

Orchid flowers normally have three petals, and one of

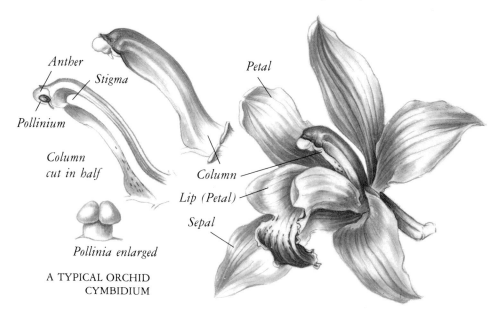

Anther

Stigma

Petal

Pollinium

Column cut in half

Column

Lip (Petal)

Sepal

Pollinia enlarged

A TYPICAL ORCHID
CYMBIDIUM

them, called the *lip*, is always enlarged and showy. Like any large petal, it is banner, landing place, nectar guide, and shelter. And sometimes it is elongated into a nectar tube. The three sepals usually look much like petals.

In the center of every orchid flower is a *column*—the pistil and stamens combined into one body. This column can be almost any size and shape, but it is always prominent, and it always has a stigma and one or two anthers. Orchid pollen, like that of milkweeds, is massed into pollinia. They are sometimes waxy, sometimes sticky, and each one contains a very great number of pollen grains. An insect that carries a pollinium carries away the whole contents of an anther rather than picking it up grain by grain. And since this kind of pollen is not eaten by insects, none of it is lost. One pollinium on the stigma of an orchid flower—the result of one insect visit—can fertilize all its ovules. This is done so precisely that a single flower can produce over a million seeds, which is one reason that orchids prosper.

The most elaborate shapes and patterns are found in the big orchids that compete for pollinators in dense tropical treetops. In temperate United States, where there is less need for lavish advertising, our smaller, earth-growing species are much more modest. But they are nearly all beautiful, many are easy to find, and they can introduce us to the complications of orchid pollination. They are visited by a great variety of pollinators—solitary bees, wasps, butterflies, and moths—but never by honeybees.

A good many orchids have formed partnerships with wasps, and some of the partnerships are very strange. Some orchids have petals that in shape, color, and scent resemble female wasps, so that male wasps try to mate with them and thus rub against the pollinia. Other orchids attract insects with false promises of food—fake nectaries and fake nectar guides that advertise nonexistent nectar. And some have the colors and odors of rotten meat to attract carrion flies.

Sometimes orchid flowers subject their pollinators to very rough treatment, firing pollinia at them like bullets, or tumbling them around in the blossoms. One species tempts its visitors with intoxicating drops on its petals, so that the groggy insects fall into a pool of liquid in the lip and then pick up pollinia as they escape from the pool.

Many of these devices are really funny, but we are not likely to see them unless we visit the tropics. In the United States, however, the lovely bog orchid—calopogon or grass pink—gives us a small glimpse of this kind of arrangement. Calopogon has the typical orchid parts, but their positions are reversed, with the column at the bottom and the large petal, or lip, standing straight up at the top. The lip is a real banner, decorated with a fringe of bright yellow glandular hairs above its very narrow base. The flower does not have nectar, but it looks as though it does, and so it attracts pollinators without paying them with food.

A carpenter bee heads directly toward the banner and alights on the fringe, possibly mistaking it for a mass of sta-

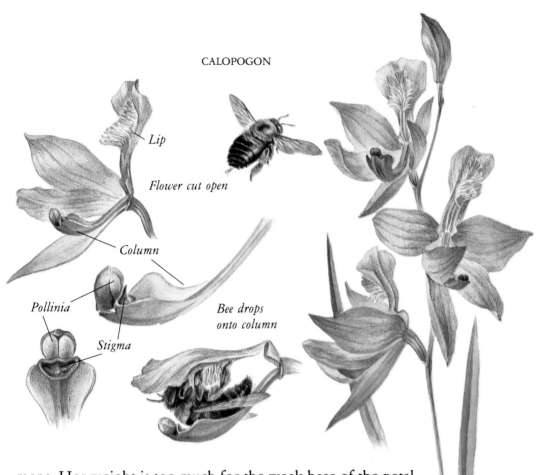

Lip

Flower cut open

Column

Pollinia

*Bee drops
onto column*

Stigma

mens. Her weight is too much for the weak base of the petal, which bends suddenly forward, slapping her down on the column. This column projects forward with a curve like a child's slide and—flat on her back—the bee is snugly cradled in it. As she tumbles off the end of the chute, her body passes over the sticky stigma and then over the pollinia, which are glued to her back. In spite of this unsettling experience, she soon tries the whole thing over again, alights on another calopogon flower, and on her way down its chute leaves her pollen load on its stigma.

77

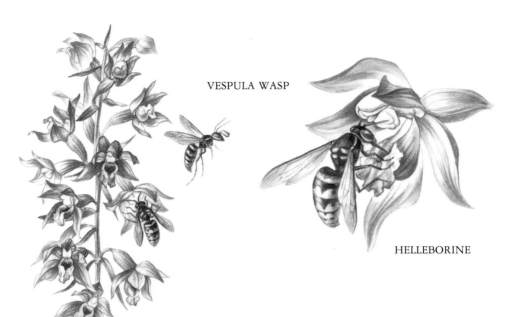

VESPULA WASP

HELLEBORINE

Another simple northern orchid is the little helleborine. It is almost a weed along woodland paths in New England, and we can easily watch the black-and-yellow wasps that often alight on its flower stalk. A wasp works her way upward, samples nectar in each floret, and then flies off with a pair of cream-colored horns projecting from her forehead.

A close look at a flower explains what has happened. We find three greenish sepals and three dull lavender petals. The lowest petal is cup shaped, a ruffled lip with a chocolate-colored nectar guide on its inner surface. On the column, the flat, squarish stigma is tucked in below a single anther that has two pockets, each holding a sausage-shaped pollinium. The outer tips of the two pollinia protrude a little from their cups. They are joined together by a white shiny blob, a sticky disk that projects forward like a bubble of chewing gum at the end of the column.

78

A wasp approaching a flower will move directly toward the dark spot and the nectar just beyond it. If the flower is a young one, near the top of the stalk, her forehead will touch the suction bubble of the pollinia, which will immediately stick to her. As she backs out of the flower, the pollinia are pulled from their pouches, and they decorate her forehead as she flies off to another helleborine plant. Normally she starts to work at the base of a stalk, where the older flowers are. These flowers are open wider, with the stigma raised so that it is now in the path of the wasp. The empty anther sacs have moved up and back, out of the way. So the incoming wasp cannot help pushing the pollinia on her head against the stigma's surface, where at least part of the mass sticks fast. Only in this way can the pollen reach a stigma.

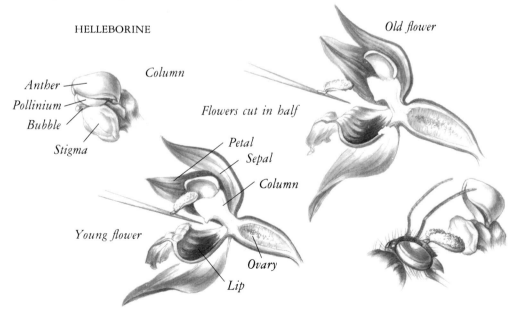

HELLEBORINE

Old flower

Column

Anther

Pollinium

Bubble

Stigma

Flowers cut in half

Petal

Sepal

Column

Young flower

Ovary

Lip

A *Vespula* wasp is just the right size to perform this operation. When she reaches for nectar, her head is exactly in position to bump the suction bubble, which can clamp firmly to her smooth, almost hairless forehead. So our little *Vespula* is the regular pollinator.

In tropical orchids, all the tricks and devices are carried even further. These strange blossoms amazed and delighted Charles Darwin when he studied them during his famous trip around South America. He wrote an enormous book on the "various contrivances" of orchids, and used many of his discoveries to explain flower fertilization. But when he described some of them to another naturalist, the man said, "Do you really think I can believe all that?"

Flowers like these persuaded Darwin that nature abhors self-fertilization, and they illustrate the extreme measures she has taken to avoid it. But even so, the rule is often broken, and self-pollination is still common. It is really a practical necessity, and most flowers (but few orchids) can pollinate themselves if all else fails. If for some reason—a cold and rainy season perhaps—a flower's normal visitors fail to reach it, pollination can often take place as the wilting anthers and pistil curl and touch each other. And sometimes self-sterile flowers lose their sterility near the end of their bloom, which is an advantage in case they have received no foreign pollen.

A few plant species are always self-pollinated. Among them are cultivated plants like wheat, barley, and various beans, which man has carried all over the world. In new environ-

WHEAT

SWEET PEA

ments and far from their original pollinators, they have come to depend on self-fertilization. And in the case of these food plants, it is a good thing. They have been carefully developed by breeders, and self-pollination makes them "breed true." It is fortunate that their genes cannot be mixed up by insects carrying pollen from other varieties.

Some members of the pea family regularly pollinate themselves, because insects find it too hard to reach the tightly wrapped nectar. And in many grasses, anthers and stigmas mature inside the bud and pollination is finished by the time the florets open to their usual partner, the wind.

A few plant families produce flowers that are especially designed for self-pollination. These are *cleistogamous* ("closed-marriage") flowers, and they never open at all. In violet and wood sorrel, the tiny closed buds appear just as the "normal" spring bloom is ending, and they continue through the summer. Cleistogamous flowers are not a last-minute emergency measure. They are a permanent backup system, to ensure seeds no matter how bad the weather or how few the insects. And in the violet at least, they help produce carpets of blossoms each year in every field and woodland.

All violets bear these hidden flowers in addition to showy "normal" flowers that have an excellent cross-pollination system. In the showy blossoms, five stamens form a cone around the pistil and shed their pollen inside it, well behind the projecting stigma. Only an insect can transfer that pollen, which it picks up by thrusting its tongue through the cone to the nectar spur beyond. But the tiny cleistogamous flowers, usually snuggling at the base of the plant, never attract insects.

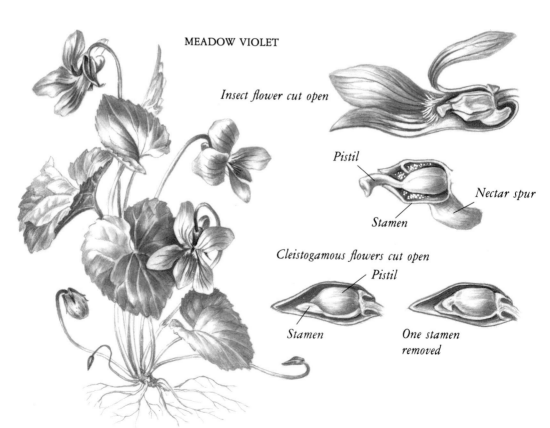

MEADOW VIOLET

Insect flower cut open

Pistil

Nectar spur

Stamen

Cleistogamous flowers cut open

Pistil

Stamen

One stamen removed

They have no petals, no nectar, no scent, and only two stamens. The two anthers, instead of lying behind the stigma,
clasp it tightly and shed their pollen directly onto it. These
buds never open, but their fertilized pistils grow into pods
bursting with seeds.

We have learned by now that the purpose of all pollination
is the production of seeds to propagate plants. But propaga-
tion is possible without seeds, and every gardener knows how
to grow plants from cuttings. This is called *vegetative reproduction*, and it happens in nature just as it does in the garden.
Willow twigs constantly break from the tree and take root in
the earth beneath it. Other plants send out long roots or
underground stems, with dozens of shoots growing up from
their nodes. Some of them, like English ivy, seldom bear
seeds, and some have completely lost the normal process of
reproduction. Very often, gardeners prefer to use cuttings.
Potato plants, for instance, bear many flowers and lots of
seeds, but in the United States they are always propagated by
pieces of their underground tubers.

Vegetative reproduction produces a lot of plants effec-
tively, and it is a gardener's way of carrying on a desirable
strain. No variations can appear in the offspring, because they
are all actually pieces of the original parent plant, just as much
as if they were still attached to it. But this lack of variation,
however valuable to a gardener, is not at all desirable for
plants in nature. Only a mixture of heredity can produce a
healthy and ever-changing green world.

KARNER BLUE
BUTTERFLY

LUPINE

THE CHAIN OF LIFE

"From Nature's chain, whatever link you strike,
Tenth, or ten-thousandth, breaks the chain alike."
Alexander Pope

The earliest human beings—about a million years ago—lived
in a society of plants and animals that had been evolving for
eons. Mankind has always been totally dependent on that
society, as the plants and animals have been dependent on
each other. This threefold partnership, this beautifully forged
chain of life, now faces great danger.

In their long evolution, every flower species and its pollinators became partners in a certain environment. If the environ-

84

ment changed, a plant might lose its pollinators, or an insect might lose its food. Through the ages, in the natural world, such disasters happened periodically, and some plants and animals vanished. But many were able to evolve new partnerships, even though it took a few million years.

Now our disasters are mostly man-made. They occur quickly, and evolution does not have a million years in which to repair the damage. We manipulate the vegetable world, sometimes destroying forests and wetlands, sometimes growing vast numbers of the plants we especially value. And most of the time we do this without regard for the basic balances of nature. But all our science cannot possibly free us from those balances. Whether we like it or not, we are ourselves a part of the intricate chain of life. If we destroy vast forests, poison air and water, and kill all insects, we are destroying part of our own life.

When we carelessly spray fields and woodlands with insecticides, honeybees and butterflies die along with the "pests." And not only are the small and delicately balanced relationships threatened. Big basic patterns are being damaged too. The oxygen we breathe is nearly all produced by growing plants, and the climate of the earth is governed by its great forest areas. If we destroy even a small part of these blessings, life here on earth will be very different.

The lost habitat of one small butterfly may be the signal that a whole network of plants and animals has been destroyed. We mourn the butterfly, but the tragic and dangerous loss is a wonderful web of life that is gone forever.

Index of Plants and Pollinators

Numbers in *italics* indicate illustrations

Subject Index

Numbers in *italics* indicate illustrations

88